A Look at Egypt

by Helen Frost

Consulting Editor: Gail Saunders-Smith, Ph.D.

Consultant: Cemal Kafadar, Ph.D., Professor
History of the Middle East
Center for Middle East Studies
Harvard University

Pebble Books

an imprint of Capstone Press
Mankato, Minnesota

W9-AXX-737

Pebble Books are published by Capstone Press
1710 Roe Crest Drive, North Mankato, Minnesota 56003
www.capstonepub.com

Copyright © 2003 by Capstone Press, a Capstone imprint. All rights reserved.
No part of this publication may be reproduced in whole or in part,
or stored in a retrieval system, or transmitted in any form or by any means,
electronic, mechanical, photocopying, recording, or otherwise,
without written permission of the publisher.
For information regarding permission, write to Capstone Press,
1710 Roe Crest Drive, North Mankato, Minnesota 56003

Books published by Capstone Press are manufactured with paper
containing at least 10 percent post-consumer waste.

Library of Congress Cataloging-in-Publication Data
Frost, Helen, 1949–
    A look at Egypt / by Helen Frost.
    p. cm.—(Our world)
    Summary: Simple text and photographs introduce the land, people,
animals, transportation, and monuments of Egypt.
    Includes bibliographical references and index.
    ISBN-13: 978-0-7368-1429-4 (hardcover)
    ISBN-10: 0-7368-1429-9 (hardcover)
    ISBN-13: 978-0-7368-4851-0 (softcover pbk.)
    ISBN-10: 0-7368-4851-7 (softcover pbk.)
    1. Egypt—Juvenile literature. [1. Egypt.] I. Title. II. Series.
DT49 .F76   2003
962—dc21   2001007770

Note to Parents and Teachers

The Our World series supports national social studies standards related to culture. This book describes and illustrates the land, animals, and people of Egypt. The images support early readers in understanding the text. The repetition of words and phrases helps early readers learn new words. This book also introduces early readers to subject-specific vocabulary words, which are defined in the Words to Know section. Early readers may need assistance to read some words and to use the Table of Contents, Words to Know, Read More, Internet Sites, and Index/Word List sections of the book.

Printed in the United States of America in North Mankato, Minnesota.
102012   06929R

Table of Contents

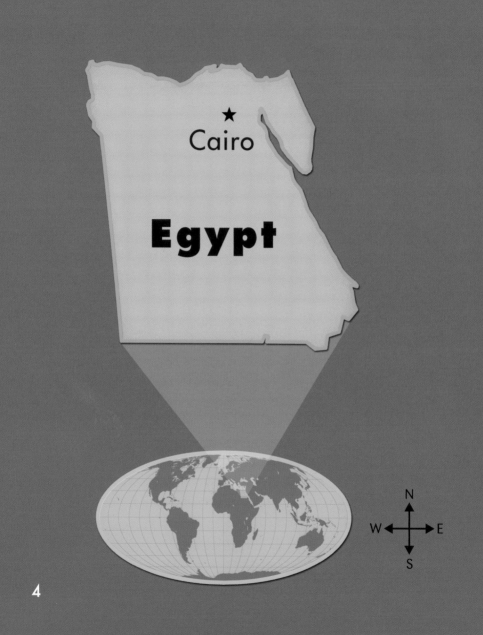

★
Cairo

Egypt

N
W ← → E
S

Egypt is a country
in northeast Africa.
The capital of Egypt
is Cairo. Cairo is one
of the largest cities
in the world.

Egypt's flag

Most of Egypt is desert. The desert is very hot during the day. The desert is very cold at night.

egret

sand cat

Egrets live by
the Nile River in Egypt.
Sand cats live
in Egypt's deserts.

More than 68 million
people live in Egypt.
Most people live near
the Nile River. Egyptians
speak and write
the Arabic language.

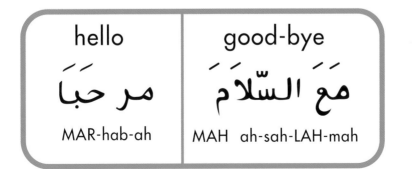

hello	good-bye
مـر حبَا	مَعَ السّلاَمْ
MAR-hab-ah	MAH ah-sah-LAH-mah

Egyptian farmer growing dates

Farmers in Egypt grow dates, corn, and cotton to earn money. Workers make clothing, rubber, and cement.

Egypt's money is
counted in Egyptian pounds.

Many people in Egypt travel by car, bus, and airplane. They also travel by train and boat. People ride camels in Egypt's deserts.

16

Ancient Egyptian art tells stories through pictures. Some art shows people working. Other art shows kings, queens, and gods.

Pyramids are big stone monuments shaped like triangles. Egyptians built the pyramids a long time ago.

20

The Great Sphinx is
a huge statue in Egypt.
The Great Sphinx has
the head of a human.
It has the body of a lion.

Words to Know

Africa—one of the seven continents of the world

Arabic—a written and spoken language; Arabic is used in Egypt and some other countries in the Middle East.

capital—the city in a country where the government is based

cement—a gray powder that is used to make buildings; cement becomes hard when it is mixed with water and left to dry.

date—a kind of fruit; Egypt grows the most dates in the world.

egret—a tall bird with white feathers

Nile River—the longest river in the world; the Nile is 3,473 miles (5,589 kilometers) long.

rubber—a strong, elastic substance used to make items such as tires, balls, and boots

sand cat—a small wild cat that lives in the desert

Read More

Deady, Kathleen W. *Egypt.* Countries of the World. Mankato, Minn.: Bridgestone Books, 2001.

Frank, Nicole, and Susan L. Wilson. *Welcome to Egypt.* Welcome to My Country. Milwaukee: Gareth Stevens, 2000.

Landau, Elaine. *Egypt.* A True Book. New York: Children's Press, 2000.

Ryan, Patrick. *Egypt.* Faces and Places. Chanhassen, Minn.: Child's World, 1999.

Internet Sites

FactHound offers a safe, fun way to find Internet sites related to this book. All of the sites on FactHound have been researched by our staff.

Here's all you do:

Visit *www.facthound.com*

Type in this code: 0736814299

Index/Word List

Africa, 5
airplane, 15
ancient, 17
Arabic language, 11
art, 17
boat, 15
bus, 15
Cairo, 5
camels, 15
capital, 5
car, 15
cement, 13

clothing, 13
corn, 13
cotton, 13
country, 5
dates, 13
desert, 7, 9, 15
egrets, 9
farmers, 13
gods, 17
Great Sphinx, 21
kings, 17
lion, 21
money, 13

monuments, 19
Nile River, 9, 11
people, 11, 15, 17
pyramids, 19
queens, 17
rubber, 13
sand cats, 9
statue, 21
train, 15
travel, 15
triangles, 19
world, 5

Word Count: 179
Early-Intervention Level: 17

Editorial Credits
Mari C. Schuh, editor; Kia Adams, series designer; Jennifer Schonborn and
    Patrick D. Dentinger, book designers; Alta Schaffer, photo researcher

Photo Credits
Digital Stock, 1, 6
International Stock/Michael Lichter, cover; Tom & Michele Grimm, 16;
    Hilary Wilkes, 20
John Elk III, 10, 14, 18
One Mile Up, Inc., 5
Trip/M. Jellife, 12
Visuals Unlimited/G.L.E., 8 (top); Ken Lucas, 8 (bottom)